Thanks to Viviane Huchard, Armelle Parent, Janine Mercier, Herveline Pousse, Marie-Dominique de Teneuille, Catherine Marquet, Hugues Charreyron, Annick Duboscq and Stéphanie Grégoire

For Oscar

In the same collection
My Little Orsay - My Little Louvre - My Little Picasso

Translation
Isabel Ollivier
Design and layout
Chloé Bureau du Colombier
Photoengraving
I.G.S.
Printing
Imprimerie Mame

Cover illustration:
Tapestries of *The Lady and the Unicorn* (detail)

Marie Sellier

My Little Cluny

Réunion des Musées Nationaux

In the late Middle Ages,
the rich abbots who lived
in the famous Cluny Abbey in Burgundy
wanted a little place to stay in Paris.
They built a beautiful house in the city,
with a courtyard and a garden.

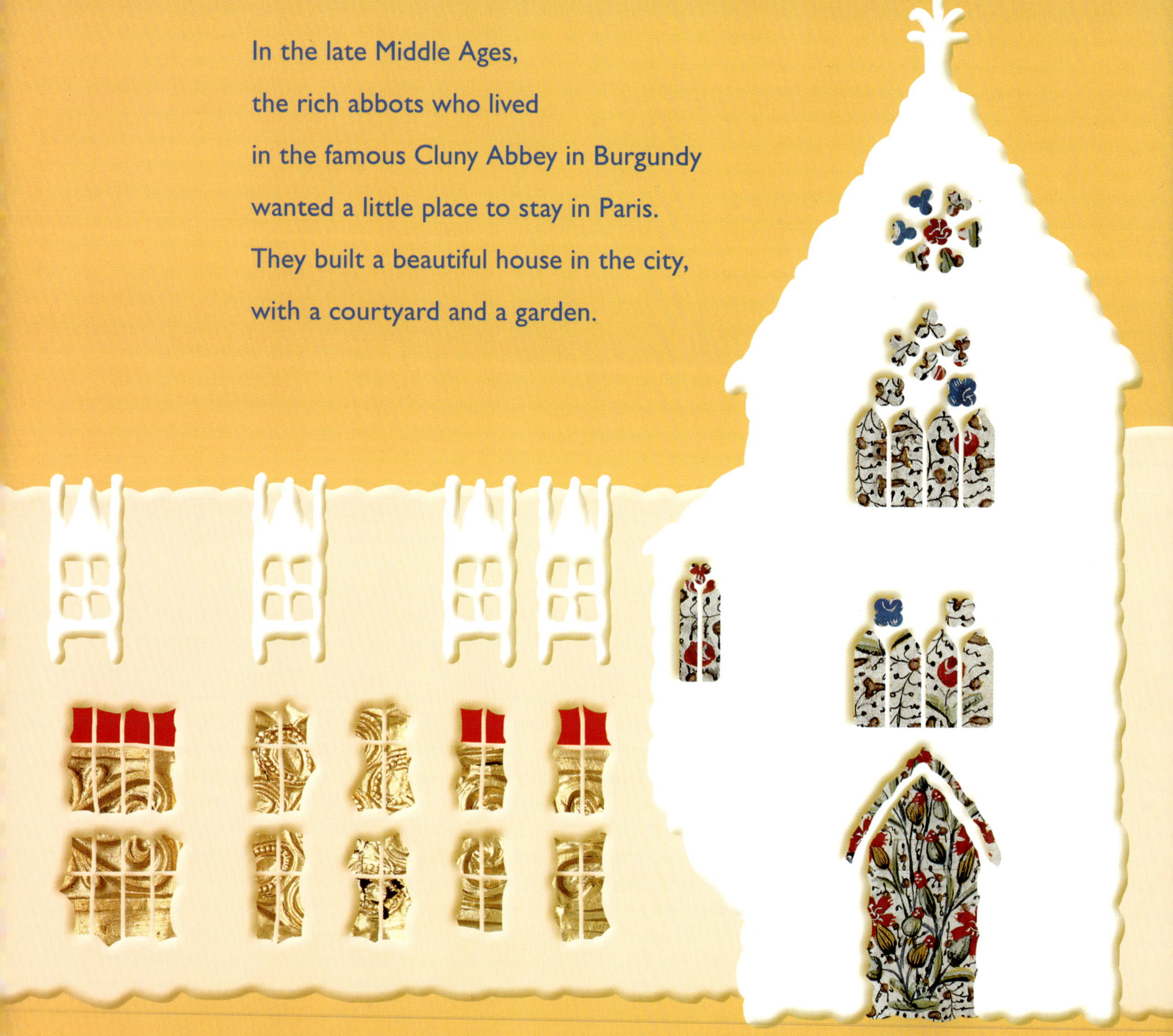

It is built over the old Roman baths,
which dated from a time
when Paris was still called Lutetia.
The Cluny Museum is now
the biggest museum
of the Middle Ages
in the whole of France.

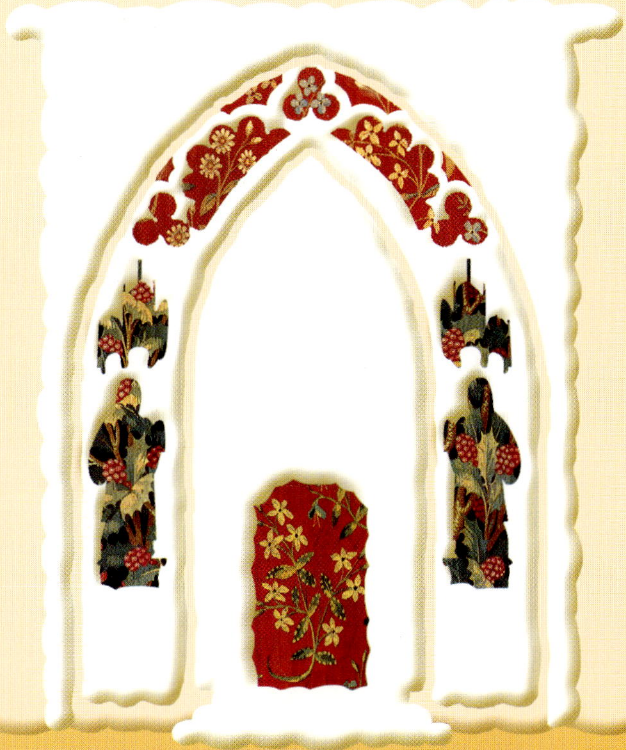

Let's go in.
There are real treasures
inside.

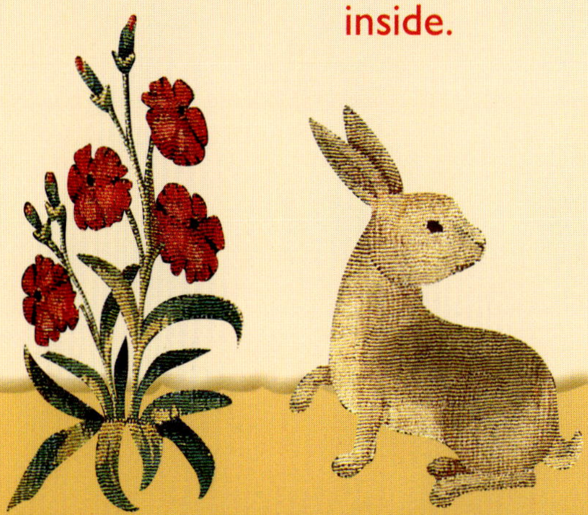

there is... a cross of solid gold

That precious cross!

Crosses were a familiar sight in the Middle Ages.

They meant, “I believe”: I believe in God,

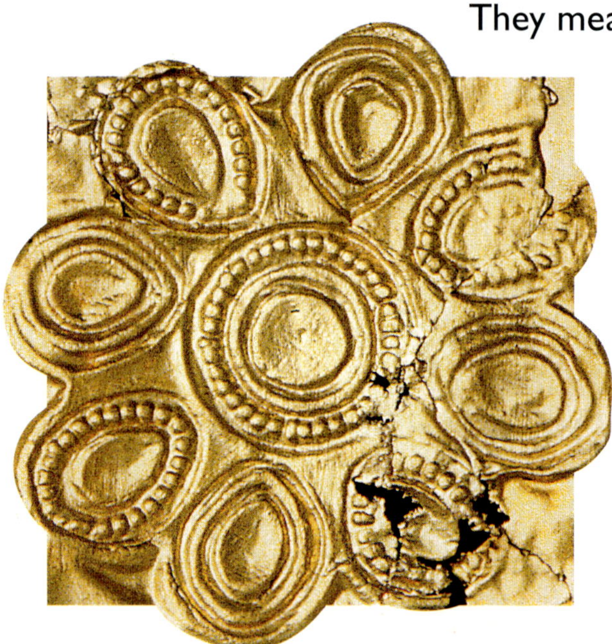

I believe in his only son, Jesus,

who died on a wooden cross

to save all mankind,

and then rose from the dead.

And since Jesus overcame death,

the cross of his crucifixion

became the cross of life,

the promise of eternal life with God.

Crosses were hung in churches or in people’s homes,

and when the crusaders set off to conquer the holy land

they wore them on to their clothing.

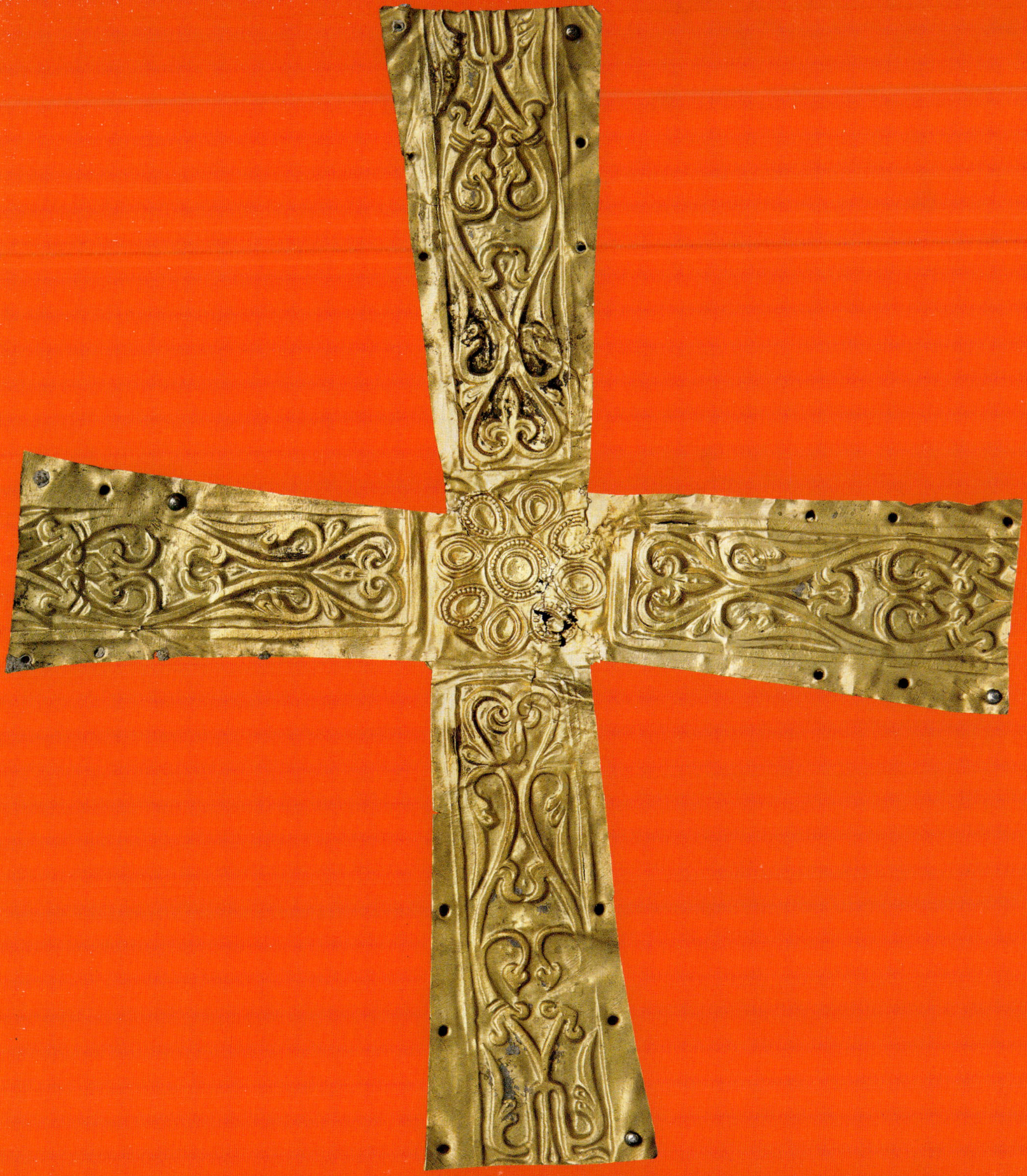

Pectoral cross
Gold
Late 6th century
Lombardy

there is... Adam

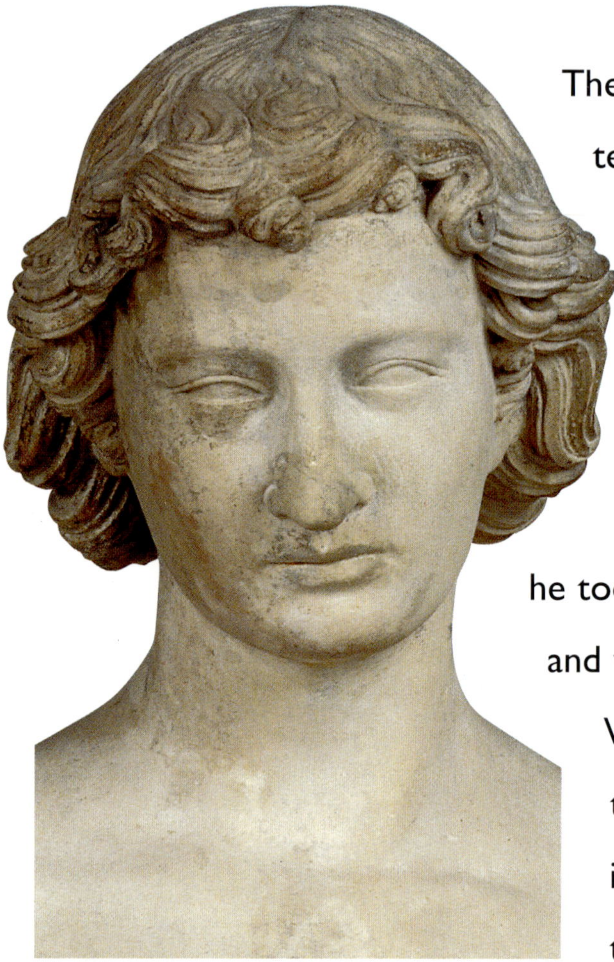

The Bible, the Holy Book of Jews and Christians,
tells how God took clay and shaped it
into his image to make the first man.
Adam should never have been hungry,
or thirsty or cold or sick.
Of course he should never have died.
But he disobeyed God, and things went wrong:
he took a bite of the forbidden fruit
and was driven out of Paradise.
When he lived in Notre Dame cathedral in Paris
this handsome stone Adam had the apple
in his hand. But now it has gone. So has
the colour that clothed him from head to foot.

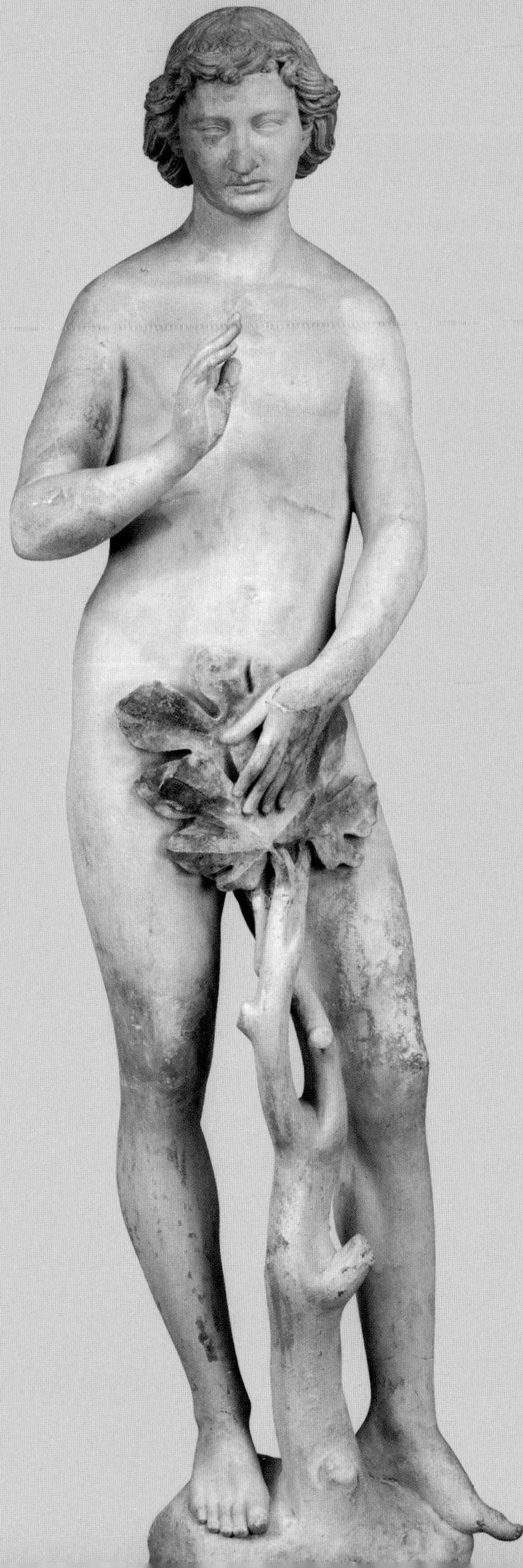

Adam
Polychrome stone
Circa 1260
Île-de-France

there is... Eve

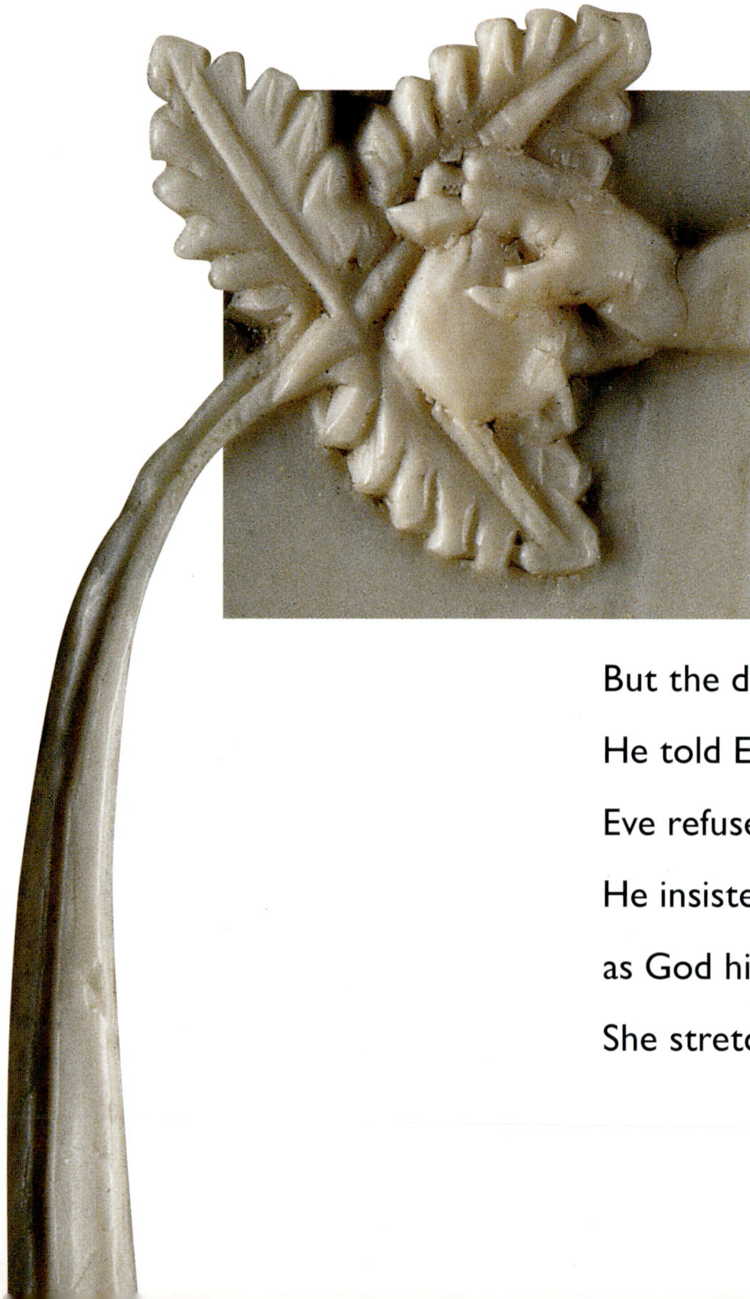

Poor Eve! Here she is once again
picking the forbidden apple
on this tiny ivory plaque!
We are not about to forget
that she is responsible for man's misfortunes!
And yet it all started for the best when
God created her to keep Adam company.
They loved each other tenderly.
But the devil was there in the shape of a snake.
He told Eve: "Pick the apple."
Eve refused: "God told me I would die if I did."
He insisted: "No, no, you will be as powerful
as God himself." So Eve gave in to temptation.
She stretched out her hand and it was... Goodbye, Paradise!

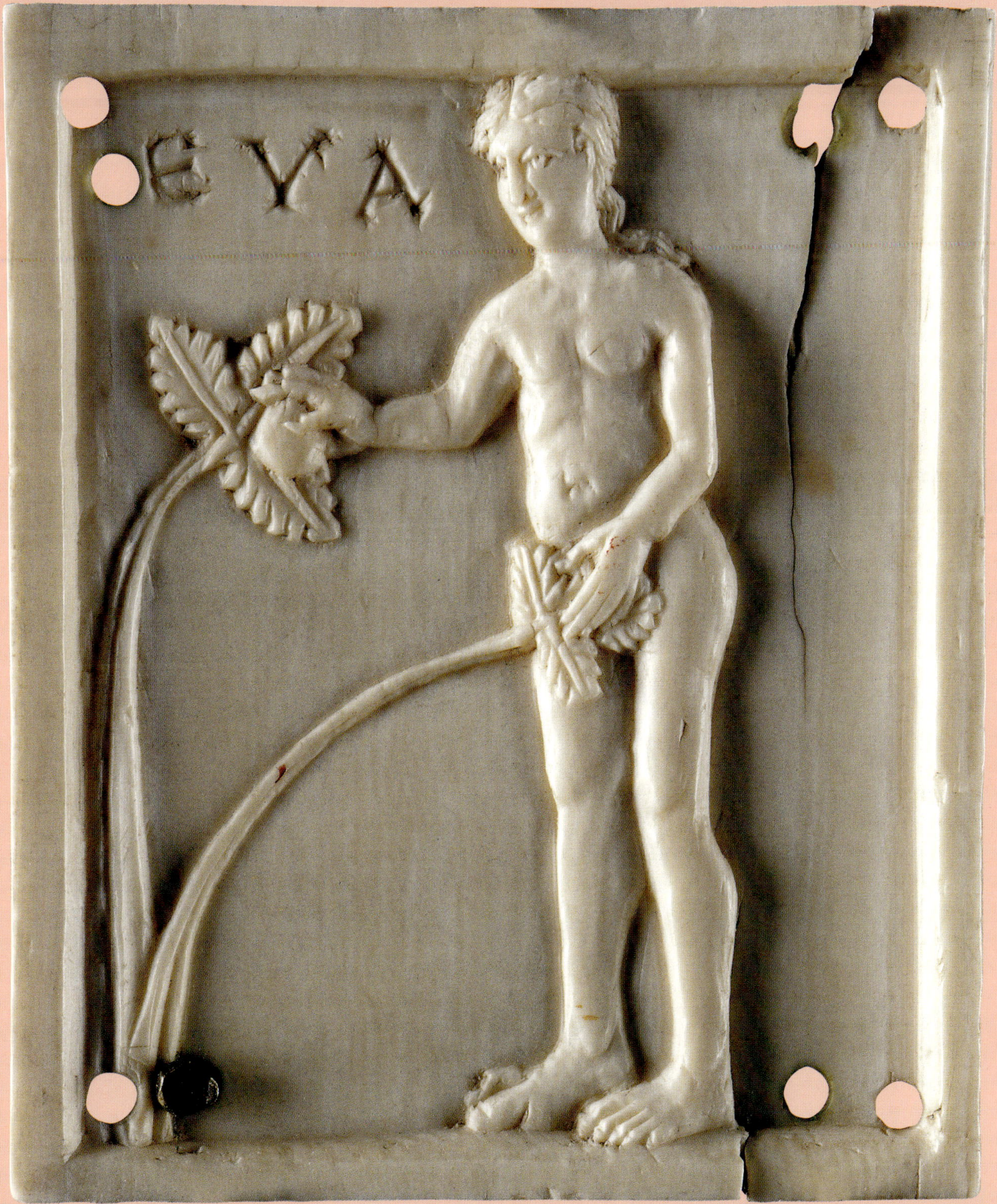

Eve
Plaque
from an ivory casket
Late 10th
or early 11th century
Constantinople

there is... a famous Mum and her baby

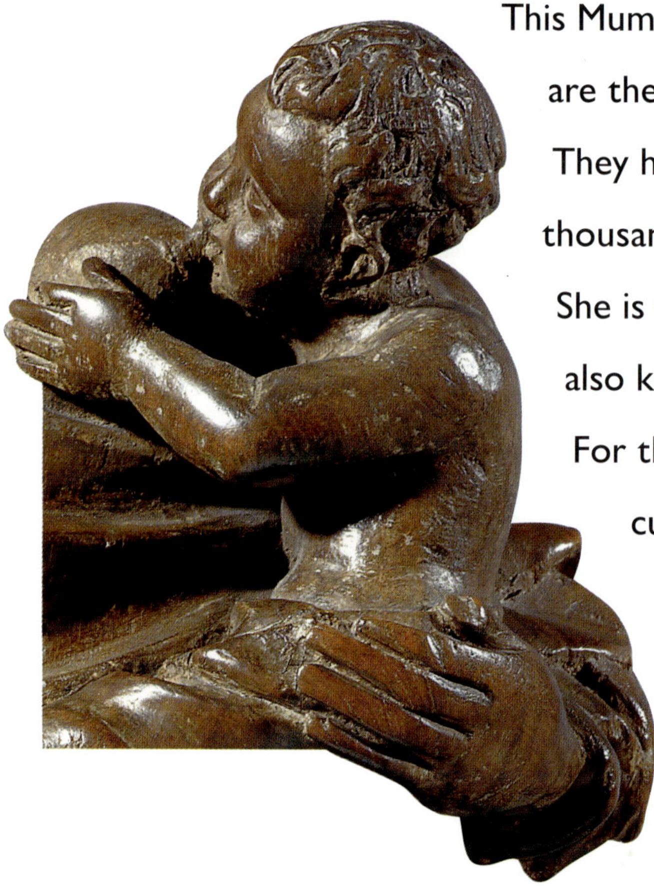

This Mum and her baby
are the most famous mother and child of all time.
They have been painted and carved
thousands of times, in wood, gold, paint or stone.
She is the Virgin Mary and He is Baby Jesus,
also known as the Christ Child or the Saviour.
For the moment, he is just a baby like any other,
cuddled in his mother's arms. He is sucking
hungrily and she is smiling at him.
That is how the story of Jesus begins.
A woodcarver whose name
is now forgotten has tenderly carved
and polished the wood to remind us.

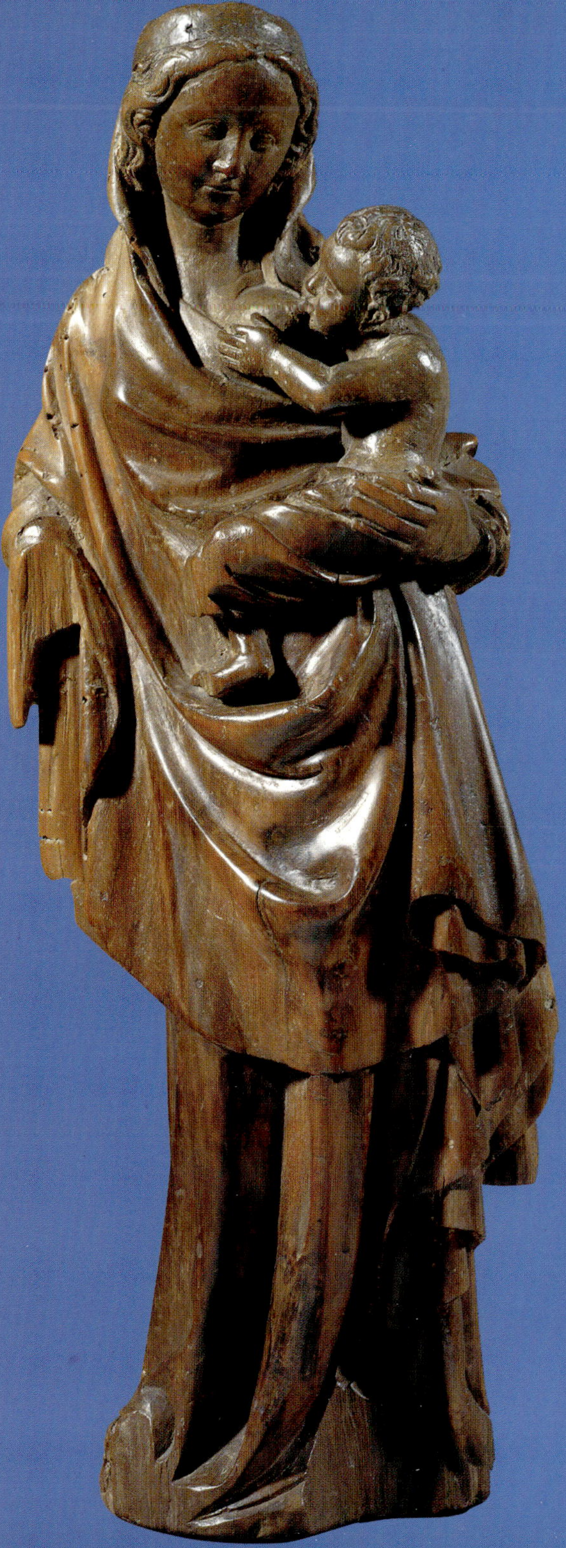

Virgin Suckling her Child
Wood
14th century
France

there are... Jesus' first adventures

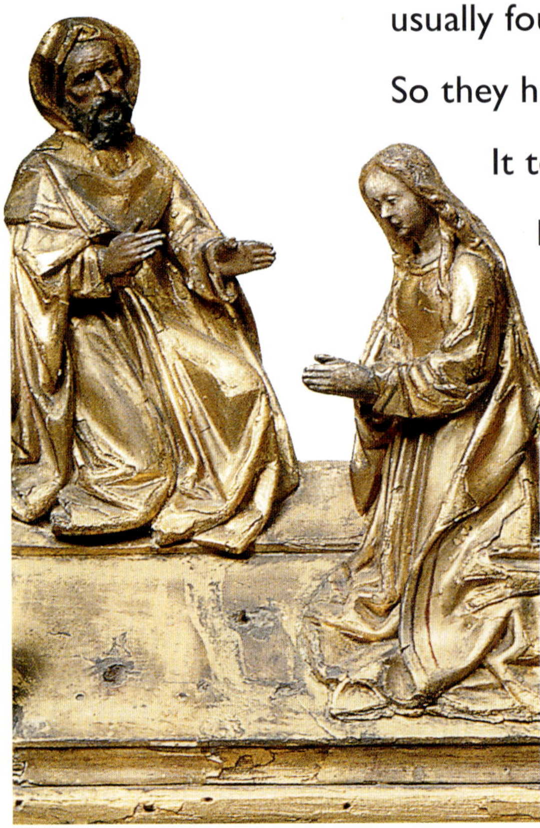

Long ago, a rich family from Brussels
wanted a reredos, one of those folding screens
usually found behind the altar in a church.
So they had a small one made for their home.
It tells how Jesus was born in a manger,
between an ox and a grey donkey,
how angels and shepherds came to adore him,
followed by the three wise men,
Gaspar, Melchior and Balthazar.
And how, one night, he fled to Egypt
in Mary's arms, to escape from King Herod,
who wanted to kill him. Everything is there
except the gilded statue of the Infant Jesus,
which has vanished in the mists of time!

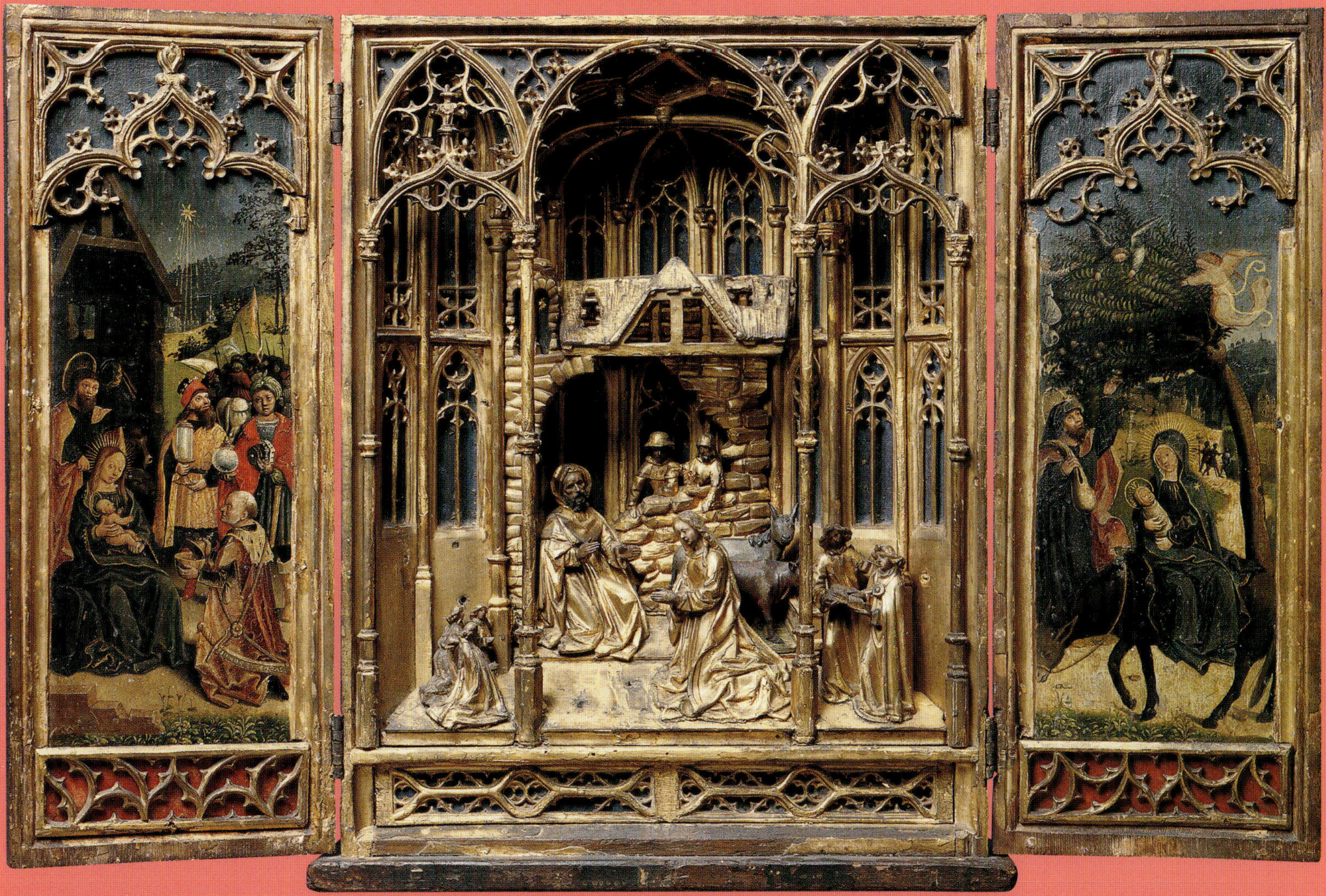

Reredos of the Nativity
Gilded and painted wood
15th century
Flanders

there is... a giant and a child

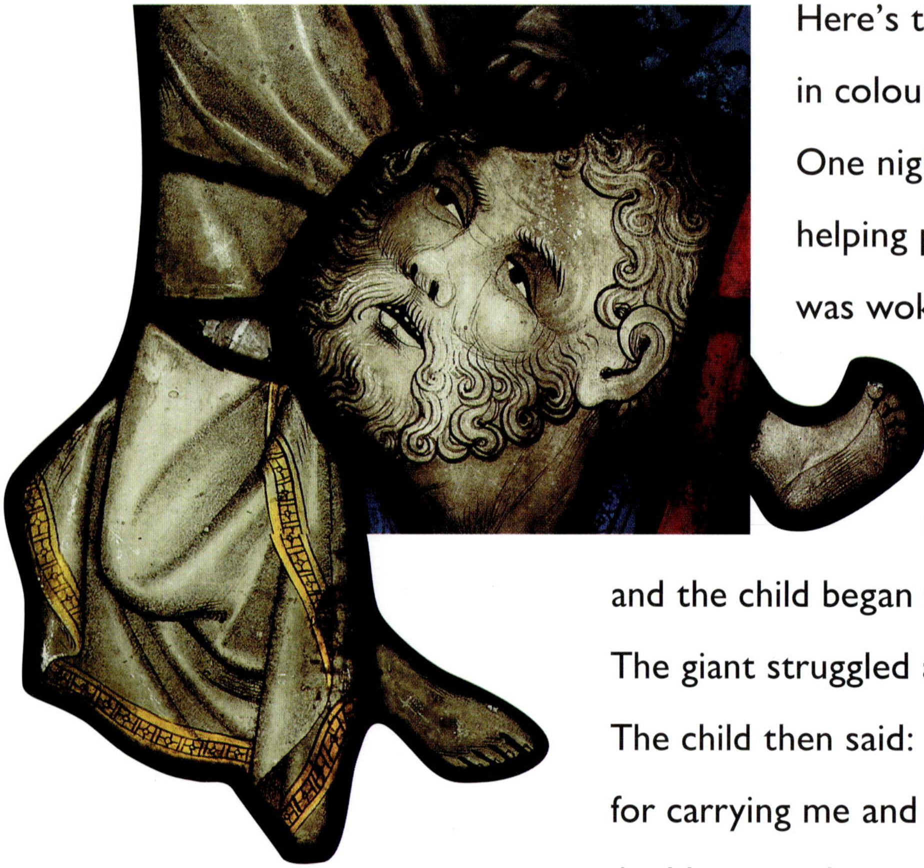

Here's the story of St. Christopher, told in coloured glass in this old German window. One night, a good giant who spent his time helping people across a swift stream, was woken by a child who wanted to be carried to the other side. But, halfway across the stream, the water suddenly seethed and raged and the child began to weigh heavily on his shoulders. The giant struggled across to the other side. The child then said: "I am Christ. Thank you for carrying me and the whole world on your shoulders." And he gave the giant the name of Christopher which means "He who carries Christ."

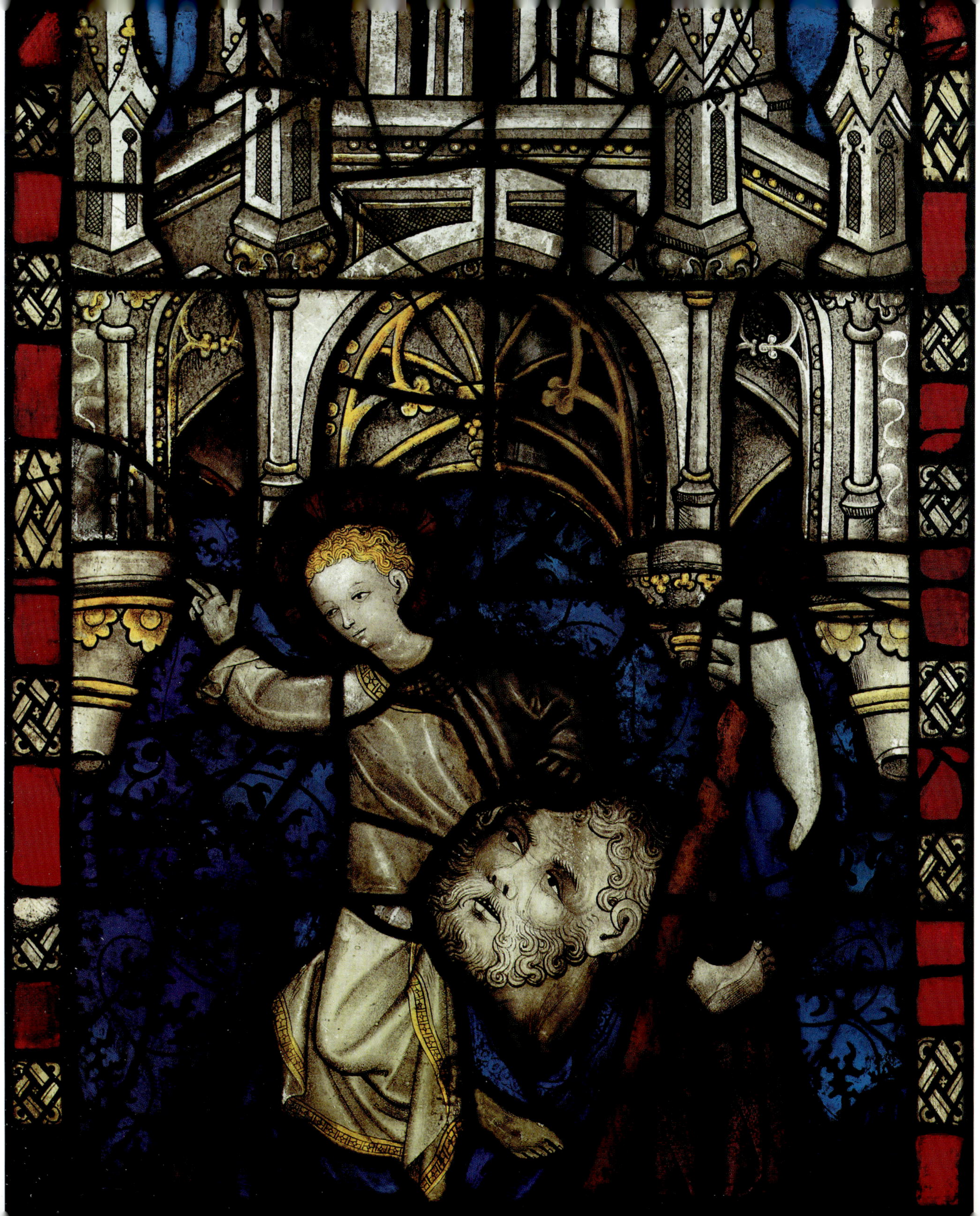

St. Christopher
Stained glass window, coloured glass and lead
Circa 1430
Cologne

there is... a wooden Christ and Holy Woman

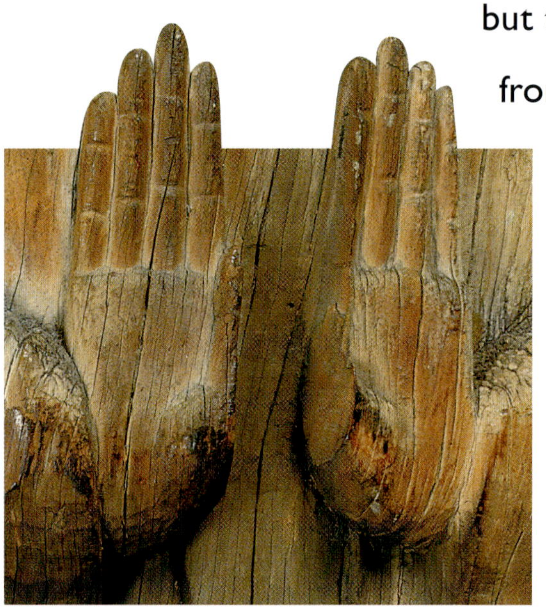

He is French, and she is Spanish,
but they were both born
from the pale wood of a pear tree.
He is finely carved and carefully polished,
she is more roughly made.
The centuries have scarred their wooden flesh:
insects have bored holes in Christ's face
and perhaps they devoured his cross.
The Holy Woman has lost her feet,
a thumb and the tip of her nose.
Yet they are still very beautiful,
he, with his arms outstretched as if to embrace the world,
she, eternally surprised to find Christ's tomb empty
after the resurrection.

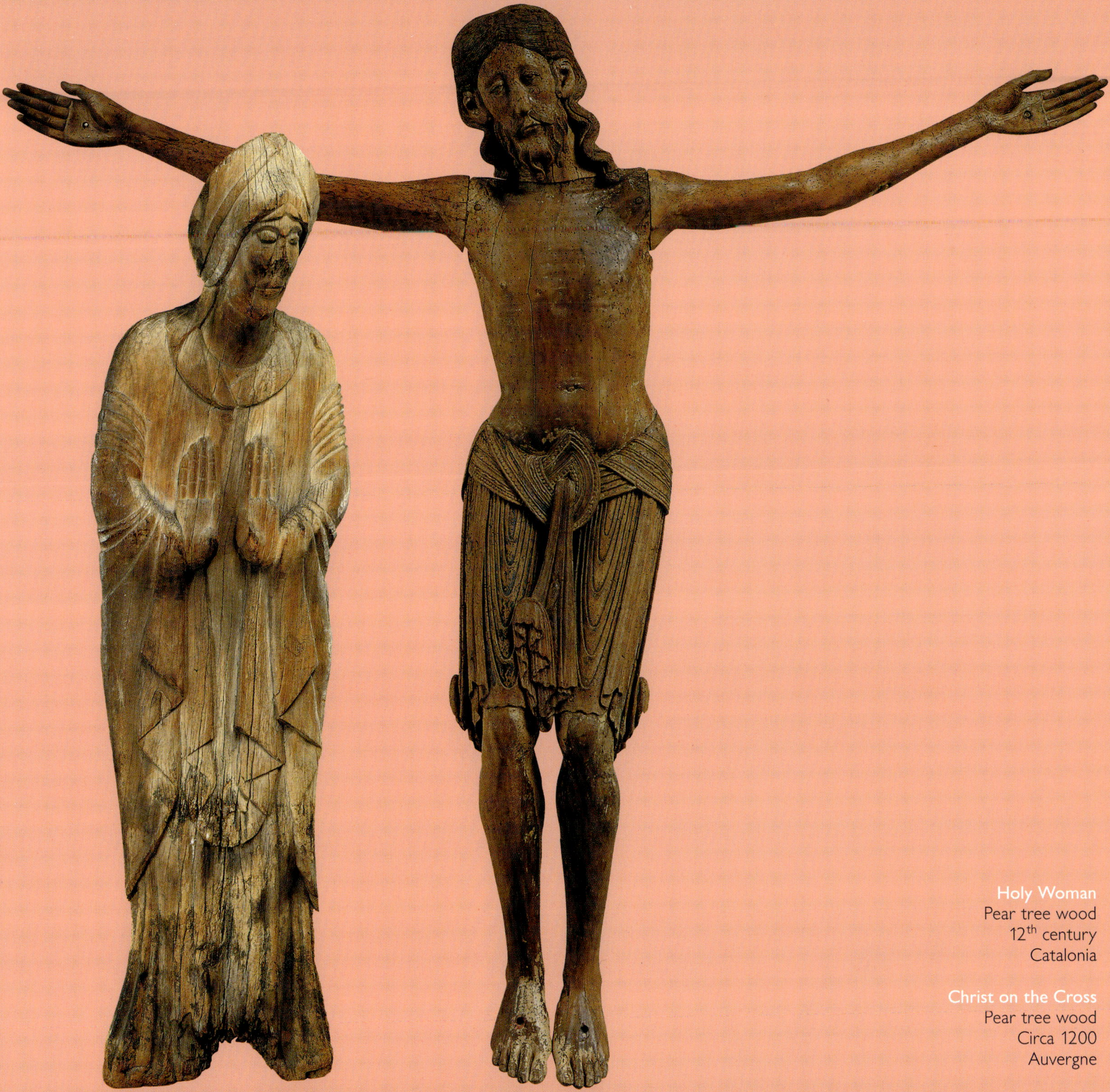

Holy Woman
Pear tree wood
12th century
Catalonia

Christ on the Cross
Pear tree wood
Circa 1200
Auvergne

there is... a silver arm

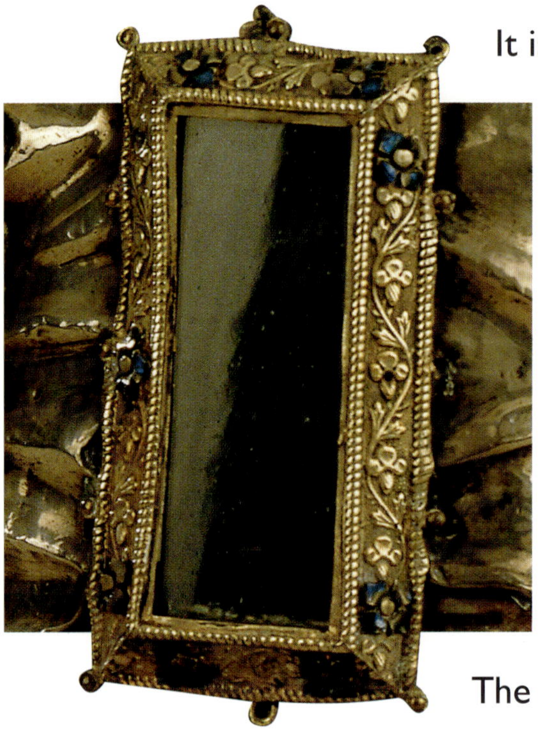

It is an arm with a peephole.
The crumpled silver sleeve
is bordered with a wavy frieze
of leaves and flowers.
Behind the crystal window
there was once a relic,
a little piece of bone from a saint,
a fragment of an arm or a hand,
piously kept and venerated.
The relic has vanished.
Now there's just an arm raised to heaven,
a hand with two fingers lifted
as a sign of blessing.

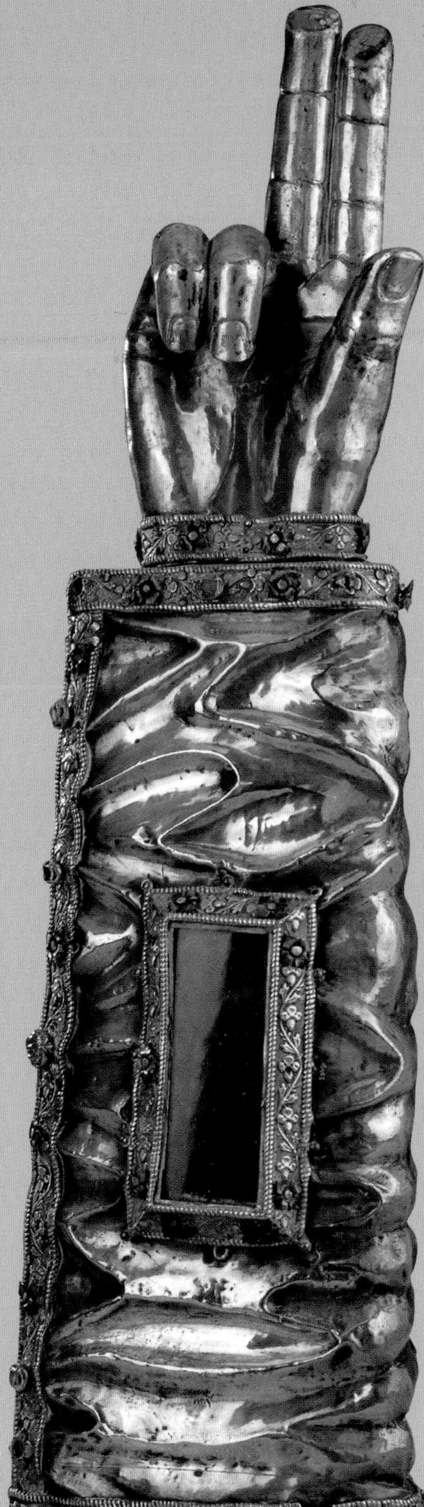

Reliquary arm
Silver-gilt
and rock crystal
15th century

there is... a one-winged angel

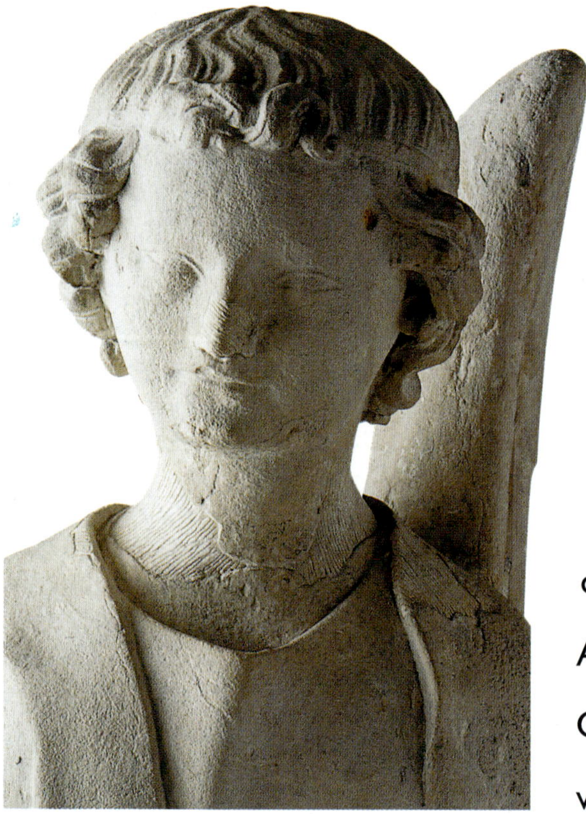

The little stone angel
has only one wing
but he has a sweet face.
Seven hundred years ago, he was already
standing in the big church at Poissy
which the French king, Philip the Fair,
had just had built in honour
of his forefather, St. Louis.
At the time, the angel was holding
Christ's nails and crown of thorns
while Christ was rendering the Last Judgement.
For it is said that at the end of the world, men will be judged
for their life on earth: the righteous will go to paradise
and the damned will go to hell!

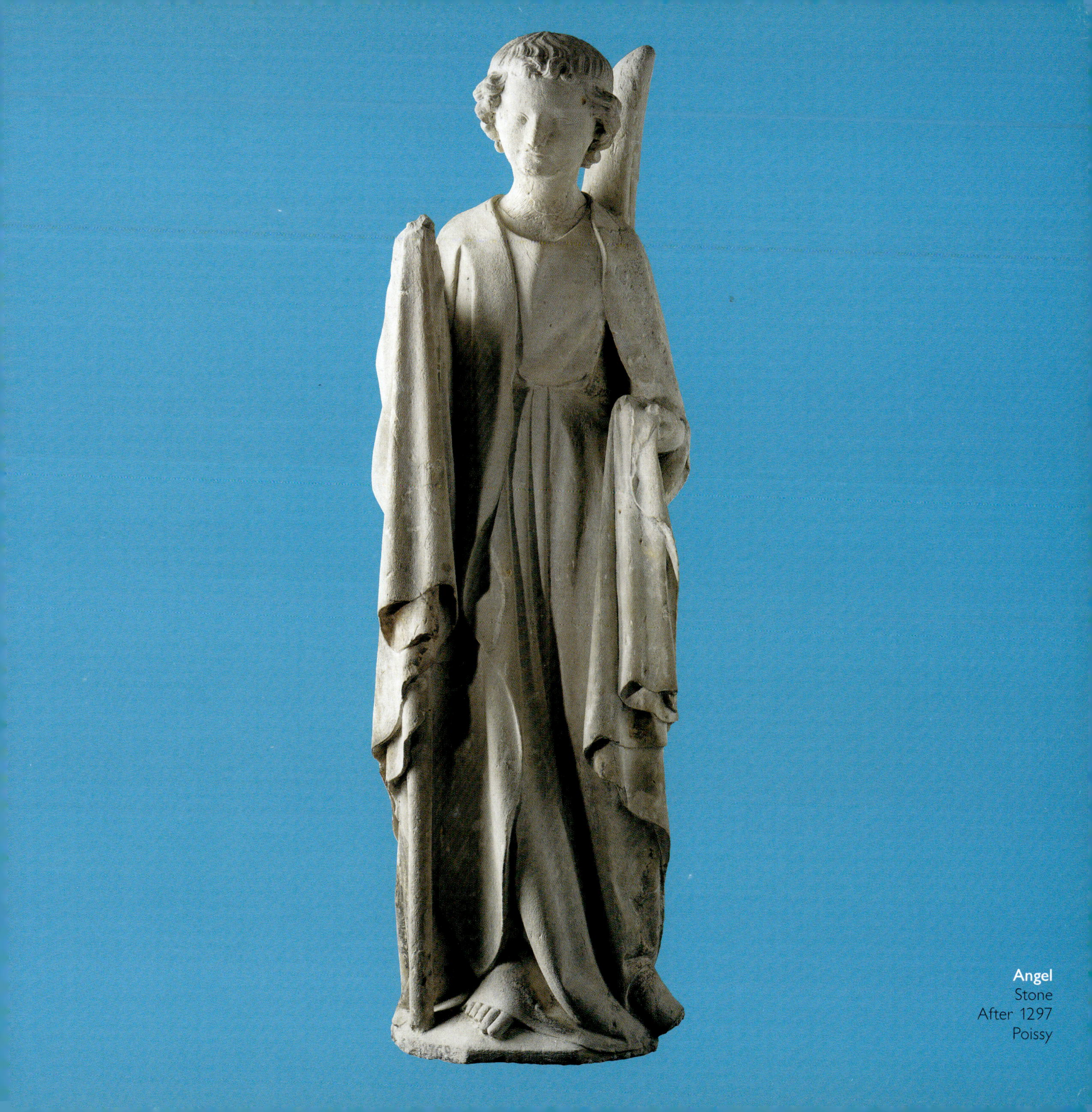

Angel
Stone
After 1297
Poissy

there are... red and white devils

The Middle Ages swarmed with devils.
Here the wicked creatures are attacking
poor old Job, in a Bible story
told in colour glass in a very old window
from the Sainte Chapelle in Paris.

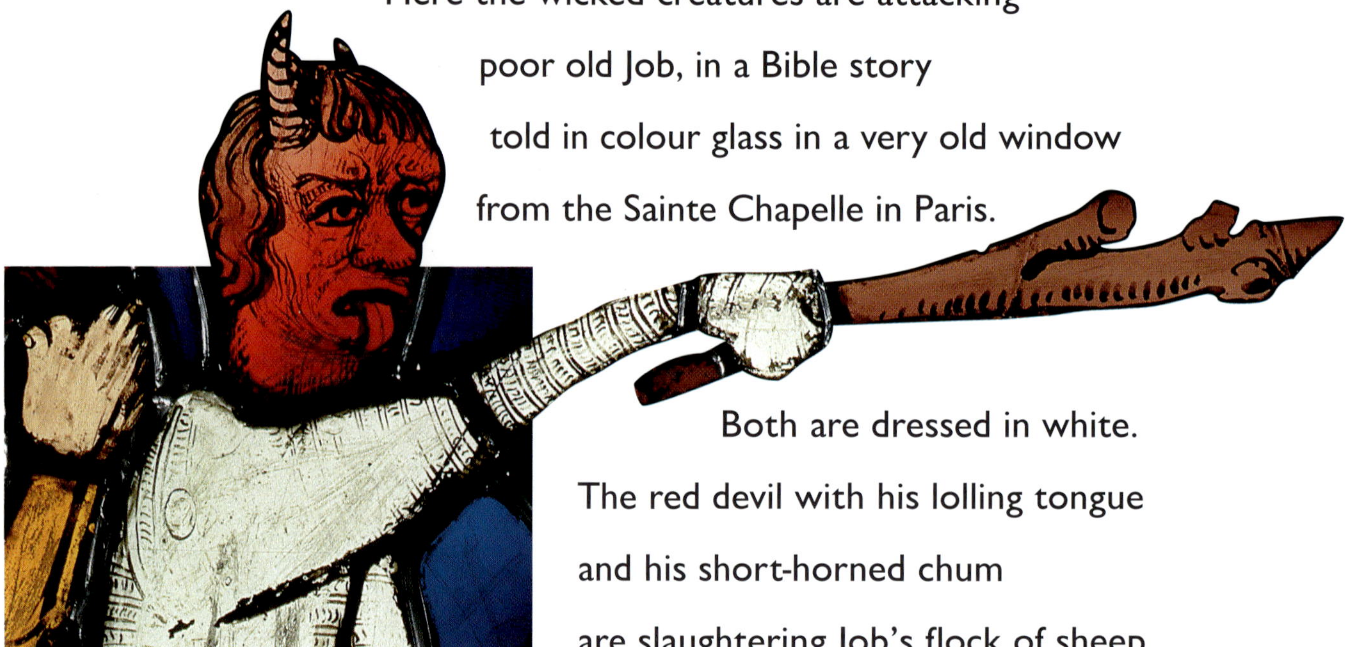

Both are dressed in white.
The red devil with his lolling tongue
and his short-horned chum
are slaughtering Job's flock of sheep.
It was Satan's idea and God let him do it
just to see if Job really believed in him.
What an ordeal!

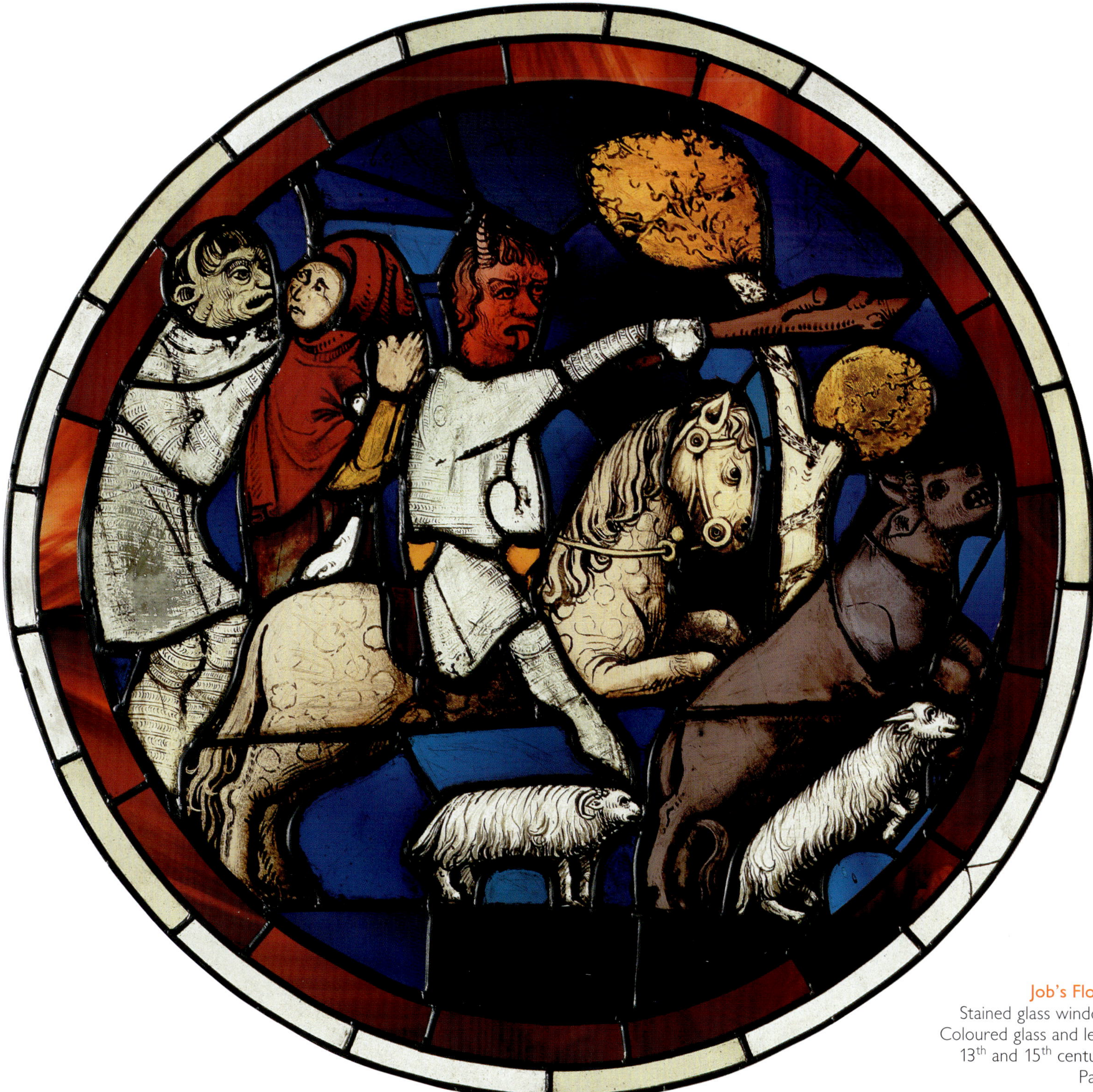

Job's Flock
Stained glass window
Coloured glass and lead
13th and 15th century
Paris

there is... a unicorn looking in a mirror

Here's a strange scene...
a loveable unicorn, a mirror and a thousand flowers...
The fantastic animal, with a goat's head,
a narwhal's horn and a powerful horse's body,
has gently laid his hooves on his lady's knees.
Beside him, a lion is proudly brandishing the banner

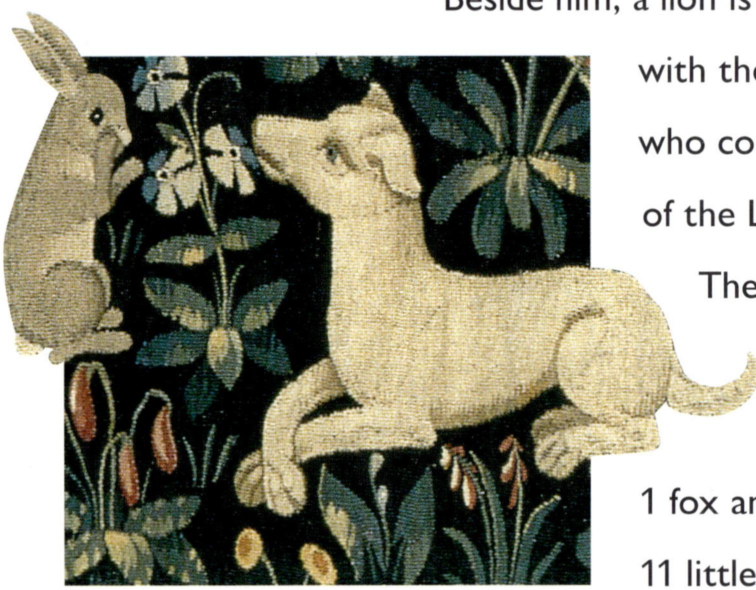

with the 3 silver crescents of the lord
who commissioned the 6 tapestries
of the Lady and the Unicorn.
They illustrate the 5 senses.
This one shows sight.
So what do we see?
1 fox and 1 genet, 1 lion cub and 2 dogs,
11 little rabbits... and what else?

Photo credits:
Réunion des musées nationaux
Photographs by Gérard Blot,
Christian Jean, Hervé Lewandowski,
René-Gabriel Ojeda, Thierry Ollivier,
Franck Raux, Jean Schormans

Registered: November 2004
ISBN 2-7118-4844-2
JC 70 4844

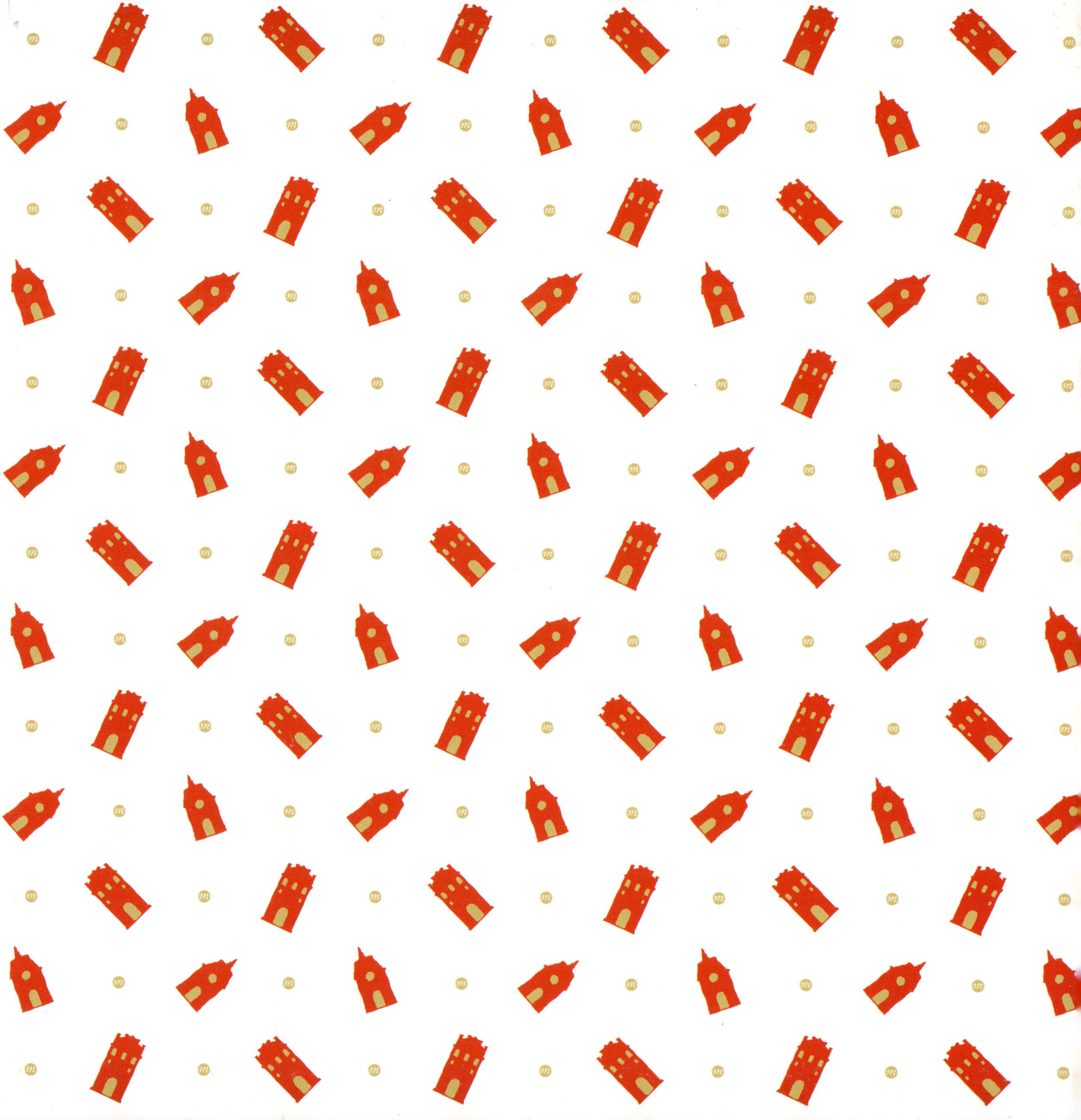